MARKED BY HIM

MARKED BY HIM

A Life laid down & A heart sold out

Keith D. Maddox

Library of Congress Control Number:		2021901375
ISBN:	Hardcover	978-1-6641-5387-5
	Softcover	978-1-6641-5386-8
	eBook	978-1-6641-5385-1

Scripture quotations marked KJV are from the Holy Bible, King James Version
(Authorized Version). First published in 1611. Quoted from the KJV Classic
Reference Bible, Copyright © 1983 by The Zondervan Corporation.

Scripture quotations marked NKJV are taken from the New King James Version.
Copyright © 1982 by Thomas Nelson, Inc. Used by permission. All rights
reserved.

Scripture quotations marked NIV are taken from the Holy Bible, New
International Version®. NIV®. Copyright © 1973, 1978, 1984 by International
Bible Society. Used by permission of Zondervan. All rights reserved. [Biblica]

Any people depicted in stock imagery provided by Getty Images are models,
and such images are being used for illustrative purposes only.
Certain stock imagery © Getty Images.

Print information available on the last page.

Rev. date: 01/21/2021

To order additional copies of this book, contact:
Xlibris
844-714-8691
www.Xlibris.com
Orders@Xlibris.com
816673

CONTENTS

INTRODUCTION

There is no doubt that we are living in one of the most challenging and unique times in history. These are most definitely the last days leading up to Jesus breaking and splitting the Eastern skies like the Red Sea and coming back for his bride. With that said, I don't believe there is much time for us to continue playing church when we are literally in the fourth quarter, with only a few seconds left on the clock. I believe God is raising a generation of believers who are truly on fire for Him, spreading his glory everywhere they go.

Ephesians 1:13 tells us that the Holy Spirit not only leads us but also marks and seals us. Eleven years ago, I met the Lord, and for the first time in my life, I experienced what it was like to "see" and be alive. Up until that moment, I was spiritually blind. But then he tore the scales off my eyes and showed me who he truly was. It was in that moment that I knew I would never be the same again. The God of all creation had marked me and transformed me from the inside. When someone truly sees the Lord, there is no going back. The gospel is not just a message of God's love for you, but a call and invitation to lay your life down for the one who laid his down for you. When God truly touches your life, you are never the same again. There is a blazing fire that erupts inside of a true believer that yields themselves over to him. Our lives, our desires, our goals, and all our aspirations in life should look completely different from the world's. We were never called to fit in with the world or beg for a place! When you are truly saved, you become a citizen of a different kingdom, a kingdom that never ends and cannot be shaken. There are so many Christians today who are begging for a place in this world while trying to mix Christianity with carnality. This is why so many believers are spiritually stuck or confused because they are looking for something in the world that can only be found in God. Our entire country is being pressed on every side, and if you decide to walk with the world, you will be swept away with everyone else. Now don't get me wrong. I'm not saying we shouldn't be involved. But we should remember that though we live in this world, we are not of it. Many fail to understand that you cannot live a life of mixture and label it Christian. True Christianity is denying yourself daily, picking up your cross, and following the Lord no matter what comes your way. The type of life you live is what truly distinguishes you from everyone else and separates you from this world. If I was to fill a cup with water to the rim, there would be no room for anything else, and if you attempted to add another substance, who would drink contaminated water? God wants you to be a cup full of Him without contamination so you can properly pour him out in this dark and dying world. How can those that live in darkness come to the marvelous light if they never see it walked out before them? Our trust, our hope, and all that we are should only be found in Christ, and out of that place we impact the world.

In this book, you will be blessed with insight on how to live marked in Christ and how that looks according to the scriptures. We are living in very dark times leading up to the coming of Christ, and this is not a time for us to casually go through life with no fire or passion for the Lord. God is raising up an end-time army of believers who have a consuming fire inside of them and are not content with just attending church on Sunday. The devil knows his days are numbered, so he takes deceiving the world pretty serious. I think it's about time the church takes living for God more seriously.

CHAPTER 1

He Chose You

John 15:16 (NIV)

You did not choose me, but I chose you and appointed you so that you might go and bear fruit—fruit that will last—and so that whatever you ask in my name the Father will give you.

Eleven years ago, I was empty and headed for destruction. I was a seventeen-year-old boy looking for satisfaction and purpose in all the wrong places. I had knowledge of Jesus, but I did not have a true revelation of who he was or who I was. I grew up without my father, so I tried looking for leadership from all the wrong sources and people. I spent a lot of time smoking marijuana and drinking every weekend or every chance I had. I hated who I was, so I would cover it up with getting drunk and high so I could become someone else. I believe the only reason I had friends is because I was able to surpass who I was to become who I wasn't. I ended up becoming addicted to the feeling of getting high that I needed it every day, and without it, I would be frustrated and angry. Around this time, when I was seventeen, my older brother started attending church, but I refused in my heart to go with him. But every day, I started noticing something in him changing, and it began to do something inside of me. After a couple of weeks, I finally went to a service with him and was seriously touched by God to the point that I was crawling on the floor, crying. After the service, I sat down with my old youth pastors from when I was twelve, and they talked to me about coming back to Jesus. I thought that this would have been the moment of transformation for my life, but unfortunately, it wasn't. A day after this event, I went back to smoking marijuana, cursing, drinking, and hanging out with the wrong people. I believe God truly touched me, but it wasn't my time, and because of the rebellion in my heart, I turned back. I knew at this time that the Lord was looking for me, but I made up in my heart that I was not ready to follow him. I was content with the broken life that I selfishly created. After a week, something supernatural happened that I would forever remember. It was a Saturday, and I had drunk and smoked literally all day, and I remember going out to a bar with my cousin. I was underage, but she wasn't. She had got me into the bar, but I begin to stir up problems, so they kicked me out, but I kept sneaking back, and before I knew it, they had kicked me and my family out. So my cousin, being upset with me, dropped me off at home (this was God's plan and direction). When I got home, I immediately went next door to my mom's boyfriend's house, where I felt freer to smoke and drink. I went to a room where his friend was, and we began to smoke and drink. By this time, I was very intoxicated. My brother had come over to use the Wi-Fi in his house, so he happened to come into the room where we were, and he looked at the guy next to me and said, "God is calling you." When my brother said those words, they literally jumped off him and hit me like a truck going one hundred miles an hour, and everything in the atmosphere shifted and began to change. For the first time in my life, I felt the embrace of Jesus, and I knew it was him calling me home. I jumped up from the bed and hugged my brother, with tears running down my face. The moment I hugged my brother, every feeling of drunkenness and high began to wither away, and we spoke about Jesus for a while. The next day, I went to church, and the rest is history!

There is no doubt in my heart that Jesus had changed me and set me free that night. I was not looking for him, but he was looking for me. It was not my effort; it was his! It wasn't because I went to a powerful service where the piano was deep and the worship leader sang perfectly. He met me in my sin and darkness, and there was no formula in place when he transformed my heart.

It's very common for Christians who have been born again and washed in the blood of Jesus to say that they "came" to Christ or that they "chose" to follow Jesus. We have gained so much pride in saying that we were the ones who selected God, but that is not true at all. John 6:65 (NIV) says, "He went on to say, 'This is why I told you that no one can come to me unless the Father has enabled them.'" We must come to a complete radical understanding that we did not choose Him but he chose us. Before anything was created, before the sun, moon, and stars, he had us in mind. It is the most beautiful love story in the Bible as it was God himself who came down from heaven to be neglected, beaten, and stripped for a people who were not even born yet and didn't even have a chance to sin yet. He gave his life, knowing that you would be HIS before your mother even knew she was pregnant. To know that He allowed things to happen in my life and disallow things to happen in my life just to push me closer and closer to the cross amazes me. During this passage in John 15, Jesus is preparing the disciples for his capture and crucifixion, so he takes the time to sit down with them and share the deep secrets and revelations of his heart. He pours himself out on the disciples, capturing their hearts and attention, as he begins to make things very clear to them before he is taken away. This is why John 14, 15, and 16 are so important because they are the last words he shares with them just before he is nailed to the cross, so when he told them, "You did not choose me," he was revealing to them a secret that they did not know or understand. And I believe that even today, many Christians do not understand this statement. If you go back a few chapters in John 6:44 (NIV), Jesus says again, "No one can come to me unless the Father who sent me draws them, and I will raise them up at the last day." This is just a few verses before he told them, "No one comes unless they are enabled." This is very important to the heart of Jesus that we know he is the one who does the drawing. We can't even take credit for coming to God. Now does this mean that if you don't feel his pulling, you don't come? Absolutely not! Jesus says in Matthew 11:28 (NIV), "COME TO ME all you who are weary and burdened." He desires that all people would come to him, but when you make that decision to come, he just wants you to know that he made it possible. His love is what gripped your heart, broke your chains, and pulled you from your mess. You were not the one who saved you!

He was the one!

He was the one who knocked the devil down, threw you over his shoulders, and saved you from hell.

He was the one who turned your mess into a message.

He was the one who broke down the walls that you set up to isolate yourself.

He was the one who cleared the way for you to walk on dry land.

He was the one who split the waters of life that tried to drown you.

He was the one who shut the mouths of the lions who tried to devour you.

He was the one who protected you from the fires of trials and distress.

He is the savior of your soul, and you cannot take credit for what he has freely done for you.

It's the love of God that transforms a heart and makes it like his, but you have to be willing to go all the way with him. You can't have one foot in with him and one foot in the world when he calls you it's over. When I heard the voice of the Lord the day I gave my life to Jesus, everything in me knew that it was time to leave everything behind to follow him. How could an Almighty God who rules the entire universe with power and majesty take the time to come visit me while I'm in my disobedience and call me to himself? HOW? It just didn't make sense to me, but I knew that he loved me and that love was powerful enough to break every single chain in my life. You will never be able to find the love that Jesus has for you anywhere else. So many people are empty, looking for love in all the wrong places, but if they only knew how much God truly loves them, it would forever change them.

In Jeremiah 1:4 (NKJV), it says, "Then the word of the Lord came to me, saying:

'Before I formed you in the womb, I knew you;

Before you were born, I sanctified you;

I ordained you a prophet to the nations.'"

The Lord comes to Jeremiah at the beginning of his calling to inform him of who he is and how important he is to God. He tells Jeremiah that before he formed him in the womb, *he knew him.*

Jesus wants us to know that he was the one who created us! Jeremiah might have already known "theologically" that God created him, but he needed a firm foundation that he was knit together by the creator himself. This is the issue with so many of us in Christendom. Our theology of God is so perfect, but our revelation of God is so broken. We know God is with us according to the scriptures we've read and the preachers we've heard, but do we truly understand what it means to have the Almighty God with us at all times? Do we truly know what it means for the Holy Spirit to walk with us? It's not enough for us to know that he is with us because of what we've read or what we've heard. It must be the very revelation that drives our heart that the very eyes of God are on us, watching every step and every movement, that his ears are open to every word and every thought that comes from us. If you really have an understanding of how close he is to you, your whole Christian life will change!

Revelation is revealed knowledge or revealed inspiration. You can't have it unless it is first revealed to you. It's when something is covered and unknown is uncovered and revealed to you by another person. This is why we have people who don't believe in Christianity but can read the entire Bible and will never be transformed because the Bible is not a book of information; it's a book of revelation that needs to be revealed to you by the Father. He has to uncover the deep mysteries that you cannot understand in your flesh. This is why it is more important to read the Bible with the Holy Spirit than with Hebrew and Greek translations. It is his desire that you know the depths of his heart concerning who you are, because the moment you know who you are, then and only then will you be able to understand why you were created. He doesn't only tell Jeremiah that he was chosen by God long before he was born, but he also reaffirms his call as a prophet to the nations. God does not merely reveal to you your importance to him but also reveal to you the purpose why you were created. There are so many people who live every single day building, working, and striving without ever knowing why they exist. This leaves so many with an emptiness inside of them. No matter how much they accomplish in life, they are left dry because they have never come to God to know why they exist. I believe every single one of us is trapped in the story line of God, and no one can escape it. But there are many people who don't live out God's original purpose for them, so they go out trying to create their own. God knows every single story line and decision that can be made, so nothing happens outside of his omnipotence. God is not in heaven shocked by the decisions of the world because he knows those that belong to him. This is why on the day of judgment, the Bible says, "The books will be opened." God has your entire life laid out in his book, and his desire is that you come to the knowledge of it and walk it out. God tells Jeremiah, "I knew you before," which is one of the most powerful revelations in the Bible, that before you came to know him, he had already come to know you. This must be a constant reminder in our hearts that he has already known us because the heart has a way of withering and hardening over time if it is not reminded of this truth. This is why the truth must be delivered to our earthly hearts DAILY, because the moment Jesus stops being the supplier of truth in your life is the moment your heart grows cold and settles for religion over relationship. God tells Jeremiah, "Before you were born, I sanctified you and ordained you." The Lord tells him this because it keeps him from depending on his works so he can put his full trust and dependency on God. He was not the one who earned his sanctification, but it was God who had already made him clean. With Jesus as our high priest and mediator, we must come to know that he has made us clean in God.

After the Call

Jeremiah 1:6 (NKJV)

Then I said: "Ah, lord God! Behold, I cannot speak, for I am a youth"

But the lord said to me:

"Do not say 'I am a youth'

For you shall go to all to whom I send you, and whatever I command you, you shall speak

Do not be afraid of their faces, for I am with you to deliver you' says the lord."

Whenever God calls someone to himself, he always gives them an assignment. Never in the scriptures do you see someone come to the Lord and not be given a divine assignment from the Lord. There are Christians who have been serving God for years but have been running from their God-ordained assignment. Many times, "after" God calls us, the flesh begins to speak loud enough to create doubt, fear, and anxiety. The plan of the enemy is to twist and manipulate what God said to redirect us somewhere else, and many times, the devil does this by using our emotions and feelings. Jeremiah was known as the weeping prophet. He was known for being emotional. Notice how Jeremiah immediately presents the reason "why" he cannot do what God told him to do. This is the same case for many Christians. After God moves on their life in a powerful way, they still have reasons why they cannot do all that God has spoken. Understand that fear will silence you and doubt will stop you. Jeremiah was afraid he couldn't speak because he was insecure about his age and afraid of the opinions of people. But notice how the Lord tells him, "Do not! Say I am just a youth, for you shall go! And do not be afraid of their faces for I am with you." He sternly corrects him as a father who loves his child and knows what is best. He is a father who knows the end from the beginning and will not allow him to be controlled by his feelings and emotions. You must understand that God knows every single part about you. There is absolutely nothing about you that he does not already know. Before he called Jeremiah, he knew he would be flooded with doubt, yet he still chose him! Your doubt and your fears do not intimidate God, nor do they worry Him. He knows exactly what he is doing with you. Notice how he encourages Jeremiah by saying, "I am with you to deliver you," but he also sets a command in place that gives him no options. He doesn't say, "You should go" or "If you go." He says, **"You will go."** God gave him no option but to follow him, and what I love the most is that Jeremiah emptied himself of options and followed. *I believe we need more Christians with NO option but to obey God.* It's not enough for him to be encouraged by God. He also needed the stern, authoritative word from God that says, "You will go." *The problem today is that we* *have so many options and rights that we can't serve God properly. We are so protected by our options and rights that we can't even be impacted by the divine will of God!*

Jeremiah was used powerfully by God because he gave up his right to be right and all of his options. Many people think it's enough to just say yes to his love on the cross, but they forget that the same Jesus who died for them on the cross is the same Jesus who said, "DENY YOURSELF AND PICK UP YOUR CROSS." *We cannot truly serve God unless we are willing to deny every part of ourselves and accept every part of Him.*

There is a self to be denied and a cross to be picked up, but you must lay down your options so you can hear the call of God and obey it. There are so many Christians who can't hear the call of God because they have so many options and opinions on how things should be. But God is not looking for professionals. God is looking for faithful, obedient lovers. Those who would respond to his love in complete obedience! I want you to notice another very important part about this passage of scripture. As soon as God responds to Jeremiah's concern and fear, he never questions God again. To be completely honest, you don't even see emotional words come from Jeremiah at all. All you see are the words and instructions of God. The moment you stop is the very moment that He begins, and the moment you deny yourself is the moment he uses you for his glory. This is why Paul says in Romans 12:1 (KJV), "I beseech you therefore, brethren, by the mercies of God, that ye present your bodies a living sacrifice, holy, acceptable unto God, which is your reasonable service." Paul urges the Romans to present their entire beings to God as a sacrifice. You have to give God your everything! This isn't about you anymore; it's about him. When you answer the call of God, it's no longer about you; it's completely about him and his purpose. Every dream outside of him has to die. Every ambition outside of him has to die. Every thought and idea OUTSIDE OF HIM has to die. *Either you yield everything or you yield nothing. There is no in-between with God.*

There is nothing more special about Jeremiah than you. Jeremiah said yes. All God is looking for is your "yes" to what he has called you to do and become. He loves you. He won't force you to do what you have to do, but he will invite you and give you all the recourses to come and accomplish! All he is looking for is your "agreement," the moment you say, "Yes, it's time to go!"

You are not insignificant or useless. You are not just another number or statistic. You are a child of God handpicked before the foundation of the world to do the will of God on earth.

There is a massive revival at the horizon and a great outpouring and awakening that is going to shake the entire earth, and you are a part of it. You cannot sit back and passively go through life anymore. You were not called to be like everyone else. You were called for such a time as this. The excuses that are in you have to be laid at the feet of Jesus, along with every compromise that has stopped you from pursuing what God has for you! Don't you dare let the devil lie to you ever again and tell you that you're not called, you messed up, and you're not good enough. The devil is a liar! You are a child of the king, the beloved of Christ, the sheep of the great Shepherd, forgiven, holy, sanctified, set aside, and predestined to do his will before anything was created.

Unless you say yes, there is a generation of people who will continue walking in darkness. There are people out there who won't hear the pastors or ever come to church, but they'll listen to you. You are needed to trumpet the voice of God through the earth through your own uniqueness. You are not called to be like other Christians. You are called to be who God created you to be. You don't have to try and do it like how everyone else is doing it. All you need to do is close the door to your room, lock yourself up with Jesus, and find out who you are in him and let Jesus breathe on you and fill you with power and the Holy Spirit. All of this stems out of knowing that you are accepted in Jesus. Stop believing the lie that you're not. When you have a revelation that He loves you and accepts you, by default, you will live accordingly.

God literally moved heaven and earth just to restore that which was broken. We did not first love him, but he first loved us, and this is how he showed his love, by dying a criminal's death to set us free from a lifestyle of confusion, sin, and disobedience and restore an eternal relationship with us.

CHAPTER 2

Have You Truly Been Marked?

Ephesians 1:13 (NIV)

"And you also were included in Christ when you heard the message of truth, the gospel of your salvation. When you believed, you were marked in him with a seal, the promised Holy Spirit."

Sealed means:

To conclude, establish, or secure (something) definitively, excluding the possibility of reversal or loss

To mark a person or thing; hence, to set a mark upon by the impress of a seal, to stamp

I believe our lives are like scrolls or books. This is why the Bible says that, on the day of judgment, the books and scrolls will be opened. Before we met Christ, the scrolls of our lives were filled with death and destruction, but when we came to Christ, that old scroll was destroyed, and we were sealed with him!

Through the Bible, the word *sealed* is used to describe the closing of scrolls and the connection of your spirit with God. This is so important to understand because when you are sealed in Christ, it brings a complete conclusion to your old life while your new life with Christ begins. This is why 2 Corinthians 5:17 (NIV) says, "Therefore, if anyone is in Christ, the new creation has come: The old has gone, the new is here!"

The moment you say yes to Jesus and yield yourself to him, the old life is tossed away. If you do not have a full understanding of what you have received in Christ, you will continue to hold on to an old scroll that doesn't belong to you anymore.

But unless your heart is filled with the truth of Christ and what he did for you, you will continue to live a life unsealed, allowing everything and anything to come in and dominate your life.

The word *seal* can very well be used with the word *conclude*. This means that there are no other parts to your story outside of Jesus. The moment you came to the Lord, your story in the world ended, and your story with him began. There should be no going back. When you come to God, he literally takes the old book of your life and tosses it. Micah says to God, "You will again have compassion on us; you will tread our sins underfoot and hurl all our iniquities into the depths of the sea."

Paul quotes this verse in Hebrews: "For I will forgive their wickedness and will remember their sins no more." Every part of that old lifestyle has been tossed away, and the only place that it still lives is in your memory.

This is why Paul tells the church of Rome, "Be not conformed to this world: but be ye transformed by the renewing of your mind, that ye may prove what is that good, and acceptable, and perfect, will of God."

Not only is it important to be made a new creation in Christ, saved, and set aside, but also you must be renewed in your thinking. Your mind is the only place left that the enemy can truly attack you. You can be sealed in the spirit but not sealed in your mind. This is why Paul says, "Be transformed in your thinking," because you have the ability in your mind to convince yourself of lies that are contrary to the word of God. You have to think like a child who is sealed in God. It's not enough to be a servant who does things for God. You have to truly believe that you are forever sealed. When your thinking changes, your life changes. The moment you allow the Holy Spirit to change the way you think, then and only then will he be able to show you the perfect will of God for your life. I have met so many Christians who do so many great things for God but are divided within themselves when it comes to identity because they found their identity in what they do for God instead of who they are in God. When you recognize who you are in Jesus, there is no devil in hell that can lie to you. When the light and truth of God comes flooding your heart, there is no room for darkness

To be marked means for you to have a clearly noticeable and evident mark on you. You know that you have been marked of the Lord when it is noticeable and evident to everyone around you, even the ones who don't like you. The word *mark* appears in the Bible many times, but I would like to talk about two instances: in Genesis when God marks Cain with a curse and in Ephesians 1:13 where Paul says we have been marked and sealed in Christ by the Holy Spirit. A curse can very well be a mark on someone's life, and when one comes to Jesus, they are marked by the Lord. The Bible says that when Cain was marked, everyone knew not to kill him because he was marked. So when God marks you, it is evident to everyone that you have been set aside. The difference in Christ is that you have been set aside for his purpose and his glory. His mark on our lives tells the world that we are his children, and the spirit of God inside of us bears witness that we are the children of God.

Galatians 4:4–7 (NKJV) says,

"But when the fullness of the time had come, God sent forth His Son, born of a woman, born under the law, to redeem those who were under the law, that we might receive the adoption as sons.

"And because you are sons, God has sent forth the Spirit of His Son into your hearts, crying out, 'Abba, Father!' Therefore you are no longer a slave but a son, and if a son, then you are also an heir of God through Christ."

Jesus said, "A servant does not know his master's business." He doesn't call us servants. He calls us friends. And here in Galatians 4:4, we are not only friends of God, but we belong to him through adoption. We are his children, and there should be no turning back. You have to believe this with all of your heart because the moment you stop believing that you belong to him, you give access to a slave mentality. The devil will have you living in slavery your whole life, trying to get you to work and work to please God. But that type of mentality only produces shame, guilt, and condemnation. We are never to fight for victory. We are to fight from victory. When Jesus said, "It is finished," he had finished the work that he was sent to do. But not only was the work he was sent to do was finished, but also he brought a complete end to the work of the enemy over his children. He bought you at an expensive cost and made you a child. If you truly have given your life to Jesus, you are not working to become. You have already become, so now you do the will of the father from a place of sonship, not slavery. Slavery Christianity is not the will of God, and it has destroyed more ministries, lives, and families than anything else. When you only see yourself as a slave, you can never truly see yourself forever sealed as a child. That type of mindset will oppress not only you but also others through you. You will unknowingly begin to put weights and expectations on people like the Pharisees and destroy people's lives all in the name of "Jesus." This is why you have to be careful with what you allow to be whispered in your ear because the enemy has been whispering false identity into people's ears for ages. He has whispered "slave" in so many people's ear, causing them to live beneath what they were created to live in.

Jesus was nailed hand and feet to do away with your old life and purchase you as a child. **This is why you cannot continue living a lifestyle of sin while claiming to be a child of God**.

In Galatians 2:20 (NLT), Paul says, "My old self has been crucified with Christ. It is no longer I who live, but Christ lives in me." That old life has died, and the only way it can continue to live is if you allow it. The word *sealed* means to be established and definite. Peter says in 2 Peter 1:10, make sure your salvation is sure! It's so important to ensure that you truly are sealed by the gospel of Jesus Christ and that there are no other idols in your life. Now I'm not preaching perfection because we all fall short of the glory of God, but what I mean is you cannot be completely divided by two lifestyles. You have to make sure that you have truly come all the way with Jesus and you aren't continuing to live another life outside of him. This is why Jesus says in John 15:5-6, "I am the vine; you are the branches. If a man remains in me and I in him, he will bear much fruit; apart from me you can do nothing. If anyone does not remain in me, he is like a branch that is thrown away and withers; such branches are picked up, thrown into the fire and burned." This means you have the choice to remain in him or leave. It's all up to you. You cannot say you are in him but live a lifestyle that grieves him. This is why Jesus says in Revelation 3 concerning the church of Laodicea, "I know your deeds, that you are neither cold nor hot. I wish you were either one or the other! So you are lukewarm—neither hot nor cold—I am about to spit you out of my mouth!" These are the people who are hanging on to both lives. **You cannot be established in your walk with Christ if your foundation is divided.**

This is why Paul says, "It's no longer I who live but Christ in me," because he understands we can't hang on to both lives. Christ demands that we come to him with everything, giving him our undivided attention. To be sealed in Christ indicates that you are not open to anything outside of Christ. You have to be able to identify when something is not of God before it takes root inside of you. The moment you allow something outside of Christ to take root inside of you, by default, you become divided. A person who is divided within themselves is unstable in all their ways.

In James 1, it says, "But when you ask, you must believe and not doubt, because the one who doubts is like a wave of the sea, blown and tossed by the wind. That person should not expect to receive anything from the Lord. Such a person is double-minded and unstable in all they do."

When something like doubt enters a believer, it divides the believer within themselves because a believer is called to live a life of faith and not doubt. So the moment doubt moves inside of your temple, along with your faith in Christ, it divides you and makes you unstable in everything you do. The call of the believer is to be made "whole." This is why if you have character issues or addictions, it is more difficult to be truly committed to the Lord. Even though deep down inside, you want to follow God with everything in you, you seem to always end up in the same situation over and over. It's because inside, you are divided, and Jesus says in Matthew 12:22, "Every kingdom divided against itself is brought to desolation, and every city or house divided against itself will not stand."

If you are divided within yourself, it is challenging to stand. I believe so many of us have a war going on inside of us, but you cannot share yourself with God. You have to yield everything over to him. God will not take half of the pie; he must have the whole thing.

Every part of you was created by God, and you will not be satisfied until every part of you is surrendered to him.

2 Corinthians 1:21–22

"Now He who establishes us with you in Christ and anointed us is God, who also sealed us and gave us the Spirit in our hearts as a pledge."

Now God has established us in Jesus, meaning that he has rooted us deep down in the Lord. The word *established* means firm or permanent basis, meaning he put us in Jesus permanently, with no chance of return. Once you have truly come to the Lord with all of your heart, you won't want anything else. He will forever be set up in your heart as a constant reminder. But not only does he establish you, he also anoints you and seals you by giving you the Holy Spirit. The Holy Spirit is your seal. When the Holy Spirit moves into your temple, he completely takes over, and his nature becomes your nature. Although you live in a natural body with natural feelings and tendencies, the Holy Spirit dwells and changes the inner nature of who you are. This is where conviction and purity live. This is why a real Christian cannot live in a natural state of sin and darkness. The Holy Spirit lives inside of them, bringing them freedom from sin and death. The moment the believer walks outside of his God-ordained position of Jesus, the heart will, by default, begin to warn and convict you that something isn't right. I like to look at the Holy Spirit as a security system that keeps our temple secured from invasions of the enemy. When you look at a security system, it protects a building from intruders that would break in with bad intentions, such as to steal or to destroy. This is what the Holy Spirit is. He will alarm you when something isn't right, keeping your soul protected from break-ins. This is why the Holy Spirit is so important, because he is not only your comforter and counselor but also your security that keeps all areas of your life secured.

Paul says going back to sin is like a dog returning to its vomit, because the moment the Holy Spirit comes in, he so changes your nature that the cravings you once had you no longer have waging within you.

Did you count the cost?

Luke 14:28–30

"Suppose one of you wants to build a tower. Won't you first sit down and estimate the cost to see if you have enough money to complete it? For if you lay the foundation and are not able to finish it, everyone who sees it will ridicule you, saying, 'This person began to build and wasn't able to finish.'"

No person in their right mind would begin building an expensive building, start a business, or invest all they have into something without first considering the cost or seeing if they have the finances to finish the job. Luke is describing a common issue in the world to paint a picture of what it's like to follow Jesus. Many Christians have difficulty understanding this specific passage of scripture simply because we are saved by grace and not by works, which is very true. Salvation was and will never be a cost that we have to pay because Jesus paid for it all on the cross for us. But many fail to understand that Jesus does have a requirement after receiving the free gift, which brings the Christian into a place of undeserved, unmerited grace and mercy but also calls the Christian to self-denial according to Luke 9:23 and on a narrow road according to Matthew 7:13. Self-denial means that you are willing to deny your ideas, your mindset, and your plans to fully obey Jesus. Selfishness has been one of the most important costs that most Christians have ignored. Your walk with Jesus will cost you "living for yourself." Yes, salvation is a free gift that you do not deserve, but the moment you accept to be his child, there is a natural lifestyle that comes with it. If you were an orphan who was placed on a waiting list for adoption and let's say a "couple" comes and adopts you, after the couple goes through the adoption process and brings you to their home, you will have to live the lifestyle of that household. Although you did not pay your way into that home, you were chosen, and you have a responsibility when you become their child to live according to how they live. So it is with Jesus. He bought us at an expensive cost, and now we have a responsibility to follow the lifestyle of his kingdom. In Luke 14:26, Jesus says that anyone who does not put him first and pick up their cross cannot be his disciple. Therefore, he is calling Christians to a place of choice. Everyone will come to a fork in the road when we meet Jesus. We can choose to lay our life down and pick up our cross or continue holding on to our life and deny him. There will always be a broad road that leads to hell and a narrow road that leads to life, and you have to choose. Jesus says in Luke 9:23, "If anyone wants to be my disciple, they must first deny themselves, pick up their cross, and follow me." Many Christians are trying to follow Jesus without first denying themselves. One's self is one of the biggest enemies you will ever have to face. Many Christians blame the devil for most of the things that happen in their lives but never come to a realization that "self" is the main cause for most of life's issues. The book of Proverb says, "Above all else guard YOUR heart because out of it flows the issues of life." This means that whatever you allow and disallow in your heart will determine the life you live, not the devil. The devil has no control over what comes in and out of your heart; only you do. This is a cost that you have to count before you follow Jesus, because if you do not consider what it will cost you to deny yourself, you will be very disappointed and will stop during your walk with him because you did not take into account this very important requirement. Jesus says in Luke 14, if you only lay the foundation and are not able to finish, everyone will ridicule you. We all know that Jesus is our foundation in which we stand. Most people come to the understanding of the free gift that is in Christ, but because they don't take in to account the walk of Jesus, they merely come in by saying "yes" to Jesus and laying the foundation of their salvation and leaving it there, without actually obeying God's purpose for their life, living a lifestyle of prayer, reading the Bible, and producing fruit in their everyday life. Behind your yes is a major call from heaven to lay your life down and pick up your cross.

When you truly say yes to Jesus and follow his purpose for your life, there will always be trials that come after. A lot of times in Christianity, we believe that when we say yes to God and begin to follow him, everything turns out to be sunflowers and sunshine. If we adopt that mindset, we will sadly be surprised when attacks come in like a flood. The Bible constantly tells us that we will have to endure trials. These trials come with the territory, but because many believers do not expect them, they end up getting discouraged halfway into their walk with Jesus. Many believers will spiritually and mentally give up. They don't say it verbally, but their life shows that they have thrown in the white towel. But I want to encourage you that yes, things will come against you, but you have to REJOICE because this proves that you are on the right track and going in the right direction. James 1 says, "Consider it pure joy, my brothers and sisters, whenever you face trials of many kinds, because you know that the testing of your faith produces perseverance." So God uses what the enemy meant for evil and turns it for your good. You end up benefiting from every trial that you go through by achieving new levels in God. This is how God works on your maturity and character. He will allow you to go through a storm, and by the time you come out of it, you are stronger and wiser.

About two years ago, I had a very intense experience with the Lord at the end of a powerful service that I had attended. I remember being touched by God in a mighty way through the entire service, and at the end, just before I left, there was a woman of God who laid hands on me and prayed. All I remember was falling out on the floor and immediately entering into a vision. Before I could see anything, I heard, "Who will go?" Shortly after this, I appeared before the throne of God, but I can't recall a specific form that was on the throne. I just remember how glorious it was and the brilliant white and glory all around it. There were angels nearby, and I felt the presence of others, but I felt like God was looking directly at me for some reason. As I was looking at all of this, I heard in a loud voice, "WHO WILL GO?" It was a question from the Lord himself that echoed through my heart and shook my very being. All I remember was literally crying historically. Before I could even utter an answer, the Lord began to show me all the trials and situations that I would go through if I said yes. Literally, within a moment's time, God showed me the great accomplishments that would take place in my life and the major attacks I would go through if I said yes. My body was shaking, and I was crying because I wanted to say yes so bad, but I had seen what it would cost me, and I stood silent. I heard no other voices. It was just silence. After a minute, I literally pushed myself to say yes. It took everything in me to say it, but when I said it, I knew that I meant it with everything in me. I knew there was no turning back after I said yes, but I did it anyway. And you know what's crazy? I remember saying yes not because of the accomplishments, but because in that moment, I felt the love of God bursting inside of my heart. I knew I loved him so much that I would go through anything to obey him. After I said yes, the entire vision vanished, and I started staggering to get up from the floor.

True biblical Christianity will cost you much, but none of it is compared to receiving Jesus forever. You have to be willing to lay your whole life at his feet and truly follow him.

* * *

CHAPTER 3

Come to Jesus, Only He Satisfies

The word *satisfaction* means the fulfillment of one's wishes, expectations, or needs or the pleasure derived from this. When you are satisfied, you are fulfilled or complete. To be satisfied or fulfilled would indicate that prior to whatever you found fulfilment in, you were not complete. I believe everyone on the face of the earth has an empty place inside of them that was put there by God, and no matter what your economic status is or how much money or possessions you have, it's never truly filled. You search and search, looking for gratification, but only find temporary satisfaction that last for a moment. From getting a new car to jumping into a new relationship or attending your dream college, it always starts off great and unique but finishes common, leaving you empty. There is no doubt that when you get what you have always wanted, you are happy and excited, but how long does it last before you're out trying to satisfy that longing again? You repeat the cycle over and over, hoping to gain long-lasting satisfaction, but it never lasts.

If I was to take a seed and plant it in the ground and water it with soda, some of the minerals in the soda will surprisingly be beneficial to the plant/seed, but because of the presence of sugar, it will actually damage the plant during the process and make it vulnerable to disease. Whenever you feed yourself anything outside of Jesus, it will eventually open you up for spiritual disease. Sickness is usually birthed out of microscopic germs and bacteria that you cannot see that enters your body and disturbs its natural order. The reason why so many people are oppressed and under demonic strongholds is because the enemy hides behind what looks good and sounds good, but at the core, there are microscopic traps that can lead you into serious bondage. This is exactly what happened with Eve when she was speaking with the snake in Genesis. The snake made everything sound good, but behind his enticing words was a major trap for her and Adam. After Adam and Eve were temporarily satisfied with the fruit they were not supposed to touch, bondage was waiting for them on the other side. The traps and schemes of the enemy have not changed. They are waiting for you on the other side of what you want the most. This is why you must be renewed in your mind so you can want what Jesus wants for your life. The flesh always desires satisfaction outside of Jesus. This is why you must be led by the Holy Spirit and not your own ways.

Another reason you can't feed a plant with soda is because a plant is not designed to be nourished by soda but by water and the heat from the sun. Without the right properties and elements in place, the plant will not grow properly or survive. Plants need nutrients from the soil, water, and light from the sun to grow and stay alive. If plants do not get water, they die. Plants need water to keep them strong and upright.

The Bible constantly refers to those who follow the Lord as upright. Those who drink from the Lord will always be strong and upright. I believe God has planted us on this earth, just as we plant seeds in the ground, and he has put a purpose and plan within us, but until we go to the right source, which is Christ, we will wither away and die just like plants without sun and water. Plants can be used as such a powerful analogy to describe our life on earth. Plants stand strong when they are fed the right substance. If not, they droop low and fall. In Ephesians 6:11, it says,

"Put on the full armor of God, so that you will be able to *stand* firm against the schemes of the devil."

1 Corinthians 16:13

"Be on the alert, *stand* firm in the faith."

How do you stand? Well, Jesus says in Matthew 11:28, "Come to me, all you who are weary and burdened," and in Isaiah 55:1, God says, "Come, all you who are thirsty, come to the waters." Later in that chapter, he describes these waters as himself. So when you look at a plant, unless it has water, it cannot stand properly because it is not nourished and satisfied. When plants starve, they wither and die. The reason so many people are spiritually starving within themselves and dying mentally is because they have not come to the only source that can satisfy that longing within them. They think gratifying the flesh will help, but it doesn't. It only damages them even more, just like how soda damages plants. They might benefit in some areas, but they will not grow. They will find themselves open for more destruction and pain. The Bible says, "There is a way that appears to be right, but in the end, it leads to death." It may feel right and sound right, but if it is not the Lord, it will eventually lead you to death, spiritually or physically.

In verse 3 of Isaiah 55, God says, "Incline your ear and come to me." You can't give your ear to things that do not grow you or edify you. Whoever has your ear has your heart, and if you open yourself to the enemy, you will allow him to control your life. Therefore, God says, "Incline your ear to me. Don't open the gates of your ear to other things." Sometimes we get so distracted with the cares of life that we allow our situations to speak louder than the truth. We allow what's happening around us to control who we are and what we do next, but the desire of God is that in the midst of situations and in the midst of your day, you would incline your ear to him and him only and allow him to speak into your life. *Your soul will never be satisfied until you hear the voice of the Lord.*

If you listen to something long enough, it will eventually control who you are and the actions you take. This is why we have to learn how to incline our ears to God, no matter what's happening around us or to us. We must lend our ears to God in every situation. I love what he says next in verse 3. He says, "Come to me," meaning he is asking for your full and undivided attention. God does not want some of you or half of you. He wants everything. God is not negotiating deals. Either you come to him with everything or you do not come at all. He knows that he is the full satisfaction of life, and no one else can take that place. Nothing in this world will ever be able to satisfy. *Everything we choose to give ourselves to outside of God is a waste of time.* God can redeem the time that is wasted, but we must come to him with everything in us and not be so easily distracted by other things. When Jesus says, "Come to me all you who are weary and I will give you rest," he is implying that there are so many burdens and weights that are attached to you when you are apart from him. When you search for pleasures outside of God, you find yourself heavy and without rest. This is why Jesus says come to ME, because when you go to him, you find rest where you were restless, and you find freedom where you were bound. This is the time for us to starve our flesh and feed our spirit. You have to really think about the things you indulge in every day. Do they satisfy the flesh? Or do they satisfy the spirit? These are very important questions because it will lead you closer to God in every aspect of your life.

Many times, God will allow us to venture out without him to show us that nothing else will satisfy, only HIM.

The moment you realize that nothing else works, you will find yourself crawling back to him, knowing that he is the full satisfaction of your soul. You were made by God, and he wired you to be connected to him. If you were to cut off a part of your body, it would wither away and die because it's not connected to the source of life. So when we are not connected to the source of life, we wither away and die inside. God is drawing you back to a place of being completely satisfied in him. When you think about sin, it happens when the heart is no longer satisfied with God. When it stops finding its pleasure in God, it will look for other things, but those other things cannot do anything. This is why Jesus compares himself to water so many times, because we know that without water, the body dies, and Jesus made it very clear in John 15 that apart from him, we can do nothing. We are absolutely nothing without him, just like the body is nothing without water. You can drink and eat whatever you want, but without water, you perish. I believe many people genuinely love God, but because they have not found full satisfaction in him, they live defeated and distracted, trying to look for it in other things, eating and drinking whatever they want to try and satisfy a self-created focus. You must be willing to deny what you want and what you think you need so you can see that only he satisfies. Jesus says, "If anyone wants to be my disciple, they must first deny themselves." The biggest enemy you will ever have to face is not the devil or a person; it's you. "Self" is the biggest stumbling block in your life. The moment you deny yourself, you open the door for Jesus to be the full satisfaction in your life. When you look at the pattern of this world, we grew up with the mindset that we had to live for ourselves, defend ourselves, get all we can, and achieve all we can, but in the kingdom of God, it's the complete opposite. While the world says live for yourself, Jesus says deny yourself and live for me.

I honestly want you to take a minute and read this passage of scripture with me. Even if you have read it before, I need you read it again and let God destroy every idol in your life so you can be all that He has called you to be.

In Luke 14:16–24, Jesus gives a powerful parable that shakes the hearers: Jesus replied, "A certain man was preparing a great banquet and invited many guests. At the time of the banquet he sent his servant to tell those who had been invited, 'Come, for everything is now ready.'

"But they alike began to make excuses. The first said, 'I have just bought a field, and I must go and see it. Please excuse me.'

"Another said, 'I have just bought five yokes of oxen, and I'm on my way to try them out. Please excuse me.'

"Still another said, 'I just got married, so I can't come.'

"The servant came back and reported this to his master. Then the owner of the house became angry and ordered his servant, 'Go out quickly into the streets and alleys of the town and bring in the poor, the crippled, the blind and the lame.'

"'Sir,' the servant said, 'what you ordered has been done, but there is still room.'

"Then the master told his servant, 'Go out to the roads and country lanes and compel them to come in, so that my house will be full. I tell you, not one of those who were invited will get a taste of my banquet.'"

Jesus invites all people to himself, and if we understood how important his invitation was, there would be no delay. One of the things that scare me the most and bless me at the same time about Jesus is that he invites those whom he knows will reject him. He welcomes the very ones who will turn away from him because he is that good. As you read this parable, notice how after they made many excuses on why they couldn't make it, he goes looking for those with a bad reputation; he goes looking for the ones who truly need him. People have a lot of delusions and strongholds concerning following the Lord nowadays. Most people feel like they need to be spiritually ready or intellectually informed to be called by God or to yield to him, but I love how he begins to call the less fortunate at the end of the parable, indicating that this is not something you have to earn or deserve. This is unmerited favor and undeserved grace that invites you to a place that you have no right to be. But Jesus purchased your right to be there, so he invites you to himself. Most people would read this parable and miss the most important part about this story. It's that Jesus doesn't just invite you to a place, or a calling; he invites you to himself. None of us deserve his attention, let alone his call. Psalm 8 says, "What is man that you are mindful of him, the son of man that you care for him? You made him a little lower than the heavenly beings and crowned him with glory and honor." Even the angels will scratch their heads in confusion on how much God absolutely loves us. None of us can stand before God and claim to be anything without the perfect work of Jesus Christ.

A lot of Christians yielded their lives to the church, but not to Christ. They gave their selves to mission fields and ministry, but not to the one who deserves all the glory and all the honor. I know in our Western Christianity we have only been taught that God is calling us to do something GREAT, but what if God isn't just calling you to something great, but instead, he's calling to someone who is great? What if it's not about your service as much as it is your proximity to Jesus?

When God calls you, the number 1 place he calls you to is himself. John 12:32 says, "And I, if I be lifted up from the earth, I will draw all men unto me."

He doesn't draw you to a place before he draws you to himself. The most important place you can ever come to is at the feet of Jesus. Outside of him, nothing can be held together. In John 15, he says, "Abide in me and I in you. Apart from me you can do nothing." He didn't mean you couldn't build a business, build a name, or gain the whole world. He meant there is absolutely nothing that you can do that will be of eternal worth or importance outside of him. In 1 Corinthians 3:13–15, it says, "Their work will be shown for what it is, because the Day will bring it to light. It will be revealed with fire, and the fire will test the quality of each person's work. If what has been built survives, the builder will receive a reward. If it is burned up, the builder will suffer loss." There are things that we can build outside of Jesus that will burn up in the fire on the day of judgment.

"Everything is in Christ, and everything that was made was made by him and for him. He holds everything together, and nothing outside of him can exist." Everything that we are looking for is in HIM.

He loves you.

About six years ago, I had one of the most real and impactful dreams and encounter of my life. That night, I went to sleep normally and woke up "in a dream." In this dream, I was in my room, lying down like normal. In my room, I had a mirror on the side of my bed that pointed toward the door of my room, which showed the door and the hallway. As I was looking at the door through the mirror, the hallway beyond the door changed into clouds and light. It was almost as if the door led straight to the sky. When I saw this, I was so shocked and confused, so I stopped looking through the mirror and began to look directly at the door. But when I looked at the door regularly without the help of the mirror, I saw nothing but the hallway. Then I looked back at the mirror and saw the clouds and sky again! So I quickly turned my head and looked regularly to see what was going on, and AGAIN, nothing but the hallway. The third time I looked into the mirror, I obviously saw the clouds and the sky, but this time,

Jesus himself ran from the clouds into my bedroom and sat next to me on my bed. The moment I laid eyes on him, my body froze and could not move. He then laid his hand on my chest, and he called me by my middle name and said, "Devon, I love you." When he said this, I wanted to answer him so bad, but I couldn't. I was so frozen in shock. He had gotten up from the bed and started to walk away, but the moment he turned to walk away, I was able to freely move, so I grabbed his arm and said, "I love you too." When I said this, I woke up. When I woke up, I had completely forgotten the dream. I went to the bathroom to go brush my teeth, and the moment I looked in the mirror, I remembered it, and my eyes were filled with tears. My heart dropped, and I was in awe of the dream.

To this day, I can't remember what Jesus looked like in the dream, even though we were face-to-face. I can't recall any of his features, but what I do remember more clearly and more vividly than anything in this world is that He looked at me and said He loved me. That dream has carried me through some of the toughest times of my life.

The Bible says that he is not a respecter of persons. He loves us all so much that he is willing to cross heaven and earth just to get to us. The unfailing and uncompromising love of Jesus will not only call you but keep you. If it was not for the love of God, I don't know where I would be. The love of God cannot merely be the intellectual knowledge that we have about God. It must be a radical understanding that has been revealed by the Holy Spirit. The love of God is not studied; it's experienced. You must let God love you. God does not blindly call men to himself, hoping they will accept him and follow; he knows those who are his according to John 10:14.

He gives everyone a chance by inviting them, but he knows those who belong to him, and he has an amazing purpose for them. You were not only called by God. You were predestined, meaning that God had a plan for your life long before you were formed in your mother's womb. You were a thought in the mind of God before you ever became a fetus in the stomach of your mother. He does not make oopsies or mistakes. He knew exactly what he was doing when he called you. Even if you feel unworthy and filled with sin and darkness, do not allow the enemy to lie to you. God has not changed his mind about you, and he never will. God is not in heaven sitting back, shocked and surprised by the mistakes you have made. He knows every move you will make before you even make them, yet he chooses you because "while we were dead in our trespasses, Jesus gave his life to make us alive." He'll never change his mind about you, and he'll never be unfaithful to you. When God calls, you must respond. The call of God is the most important call you will ever receive in your life, so do not miss it.

John 6:37: "All those the Father gives me will come to me, and whoever comes to me I will never drive away."

There is no doubt that there is a major call from heaven in these days to draw near to Jesus. I believe if there was ever a time to come to him, NOW is the time. In 2 Corinthians 6:2, it says that NOW is the time of salvation, not tomorrow, not next week, but NOW. When God calls, there must be an immediate response to COME. God is beckoning his people to come away with him and leave behind everything and anything that has been hindering them. Look at Levi in Luke 5:27. When Jesus saw him and said, "Follow me," he immediately left all, rose up, and followed Him. There was no hesitation or procrastination. he just left everything behind and followed Jesus. He was a tax collector, who was labeled as one of the worse sinners, according to the religious leaders. He was doing his job, making money, and living life the way he felt he should live it, and Jesus came along and drew him. I am amazed that Jesus drew him, but I am so much more amazed how quickly he left everything and followed. Coming to Jesus is not a one-time event! It is an everyday lifestyle. You cannot merely say that you "came to Jesus." You must be coming to Jesus daily. There must be an initial come, but you must be in pursuit of him daily. Therefore,

Levi "followed" him. He didn't just say, "Jesus, I accept you." He dropped everything that was valuable to him and pursued the very one who persuade him.

We now live in a generation that makes so many excuses on why they cannot follow the Lord with all of their heart. It is not enough to follow Jesus and hold on to things you know displease him.

Going to church does not mean you follow Jesus.

Listening to worship music does not mean you follow Jesus.

Being in ministry does not even mean you follow Jesus.

When you come to the Lord, you make an absolute dedication to HIM and HIM only. You do not come to the Lord because of what he has or what he can do for you. You come to him because of who he is. Levi was a man dedicated to money and his job, but when Jesus came, he did not offer Levi a better job or more money. He simply offered him himself, and he came. I have met so many people who serve the Lord, and the only thing they can talk about when it comes to God is the things he can do rather than who he is. They speak more of the hand of God rather than the heart of God, and we cannot be a people who seek his gifts and miss his heart. Levi was not the only one who left everything to follow Jesus. When you go back to Luke 5, Jesus sits in the boat of Peter and ministers. After Jesus is done ministering to Peter and his brother, verse 11 says, "They had brought their boats to land, they forsook all and followed him." *Forsook* means to completely abandon! God is raising up a people who have abandoned everything to pursue Jesus. They have nothing to go back to. He has become their all and all.

* * *

CHAPTER 4

Guard Your Heart

There are avenues and tunnels that lead to your soul and heart that are mainly known as gates. All of the information around you, from the voices of the people to the movies that you watch, the music you listen to, the atmospheres you walk into, and everything you see with your natural eyes. The eyes and ears just happen to be the two most important gates that need to be guarded at all costs. Whether you believe it or not, whatever comes through your eyes and ears goes straight to your soul and can alter and change the course of your life. Whatever you give your full attention to will eventually direct how you see life and who you are at the core. How many times have you watched a movie, YouTube video, or documentary that impacts you in such a way that you begin thinking about it all day? How many times have you watched something that shows you the poverty and destruction in the world, and while you're watching it, it begins to bring a deep heaviness over you, causing you to see life completely differently? This is how information travels to the soul and heart of a person through what we see with our eyes and hear with our ears. How many times have you heard a negative conversation concerning a specific topic, world event, or person and you leave the conversation with different perspectives or points of view concerning that person or world event? Why? Because whatever you lend your ear to has the ability to control how you think. The only protection from this is the beautiful wisdom and guidance of the Holy Spirit who will warn you when something isn't right and when you should completely stop conversations, walk away, or turn off something that violates your relationship with him. This is why it is important to follow what Proverbs says, "Above all else guard your heart because out of it flows the type of life you will live." It doesn't matter how perfect your church attendance is or how much you post on social media about God. If you don't guard your heart, you will eventually live a life contrary to the word of the Lord and what God has planned for your life. We all know that the devil is a deceiver, but one thing you need to keep in mind is that his sneaky and subtle ways can trick and deceive the greatest of us just by attacking our heart. Yes, he is a defeated foe who has no power over true believers who know who they are, but the question is, have you truly allowed God to take full occupation in your heart? Because if your heart is divided, every chance the enemy gets, he will take a shot at your heart to corrupt how you think and who you are. But the scariest way you need to be aware of is when he does it and you don't even know that he's doing it. He will slip in anger, frustration, feelings of defeat, depression, stress, hatred, bitterness, unforgiveness, sexual immorality, bad habits, or even unbelief and doubt toward God. These are all darts and attacks that the enemy uses to destroy your heart because he knows if he can get your heart, he can get your life. Jesus speaks so beautifully concerning the heart in Luke 6:45: "A good man brings good things out of the good stored up in his heart, and an evil man brings evil things out of the evil stored up in his heart. For the mouth speaks what the heart is full of."

When you look at the mind in the Bible, it speaks about the mind and heart almost interchangeably because the mind and heart are connected. Whatever your heart is full of comes through your thinking and then out of your mouth. This is why when you look at someone who drinks heavily, they end up saying things while drunk that they would never say while sober because subconsciously, they blurt out everything hidden in the heart without a stable mind to filter it. So when you look at the scheme and tactics of the enemy, he many times works his way into your thinking so he can place seeds in your heart that eventually grow roots deep down and produce bad fruit through your life. If the enemy is trying to produce offense in your life, all he needs to do is grab your ear long enough for you to hear someone say something you don't like so it can process through your thinking, and the moment you accept that thought, it gets planted in your heart, eventually creating something called a stronghold. This is the same concept used with confusion, depression and sexual immorality, and many other sins that come through images, videos, and conversations. A stronghold is something that is strongly fortified, defended, or upheld. The only way something can get so deep down inside of you that it becomes strong enough to take root is that you first accept it. Acceptance gives power to what controls your heart, mind, and life. When someone buys a security system to protect their home, they buy it with the intention to protect them against intruders so that the only ones allowed in have security clearance or have been invited in. The enemy does not have the power to break the security system of the Holy Spirit within you; you must give him access. Just because something becomes overwhelming does not mean you have to let it into your heart. Many times I walk into a room with people and begin to feel many different atmospheres because the heart also projects atmospheres that can control or attack others. Normally, when I walk into a room, I identify what is acceptable and what is not the moment I engage in conversation because I know that if I open myself up completely, people have the ability to dump on me what's inside of them. We are called to change atmospheres, not be controlled by them. Many sincere Christians walk into places feeling great and filled with the spirit of God, but because they do not guard their hearts, they leave with all types of weights and attachments. In 2 Corinthians 10:3–5, it says, "For the weapons of our warfare are not of the flesh but have divine power to destroy strongholds. We destroy arguments and every lofty opinion raised against the knowledge of God, and take every thought captive to obey Christ." We don't use the same weapons as the world does. We have the power of Christ inside of us to destroy every idea, thought, or argument that tries to sneak inside of our hearts. We now live in a social media–driven world, where offense and discouragement don't merely come through face-to-face encounters but also through what we see on our phones and computers. Christian maturity is being able to see something you disagree with or an attack against you and bring it to God before you allow the offense to take root in your heart. But because of the demonic need of acceptance and retaliation, many people don't take it to God but instead let it replay inside of their hearts and minds until it controls how they think and move. This is a diabolic plot from the enemy to trap believers and keep them from living how they were created to live. Social media can be a major blessing, but to "most," it has become a major stronghold, stumbling block, and idol. Idolatry is not something that happens on the outside but what happens in the inside. Jesus says in Matthew 15:19, "For out of the heart come evil thoughts—murder, adultery, sexual immorality, theft, false testimony, slander." It all begins inside the heart. This is why when you look at someone who falls into adultery or immorality, pretty much everyone looks at what happened without first considering what this person has been keeping in their hearts for a while <u>before</u> it came out. You don't just fall into a huge trap like that. It's a slow walk in the wrong direction. It's when the person thinks about it here and there before it becomes a reality in their life. This is why Jesus says you don't even need to commit the act of adultery. All it takes is for you to look at a woman lustfully, and you have already committed the sin inside of your heart. Because God is the one who sees and weighs the intentions of the heart, and he cares more about what's in you than what's happening on the outside. Jesus loves you and will forgive, but he also has a standard, and his goal is to cleanse your heart. He also wants to take complete residence.

If you were inside a small room with about one hundred people, shoulder to shoulder, not even being able to move, and there was a knock at the door, would you be able to let them in? Well, of course not. Why? Because the room is already full and has no room for anyone else. This is exactly how God wants to fill your heart, until you have absolutely no room for anything else. Proverb tells us that the issues of life come from our hearts. They really don't come from all the things we think they come from. Every world affair originates in the heart of the people. This is how so many fall victim to attacks. They are more aware of what's happening in the world and what's coming against them than who Christ is in their lives. When the Holy Spirit becomes more real to you than everything around you, you become more conscious and aware of him. Your awareness of the Holy Spirit will protect you from any and every attack.

Spending time with the Lord will always be the most important for spiritual growth, and it is also the fuel, energy, and foundation of your Christian faith. In our world today, especially in America, we have adopted a strange idea that you don't have to spend time with Jesus and that attending church every Sunday and doing Christian things while wearing Christian T-shirts is enough. This is not only insane but also dangerous for a believer to believe that they can soak up the world and the things of God at the same time without an actual relationship with Jesus and expect to make it. Time with the Lord is not a principle or a formula. It's literally ministering to the Lord from the depths of your heart, and he, in turn, fills your heart and soul with himself. Although you are not saved by works, you must have a lifestyle that models the lifestyle of Jesus. Even Jesus had to go away in secret many times through the scriptures to be alone with the father. The secret place with God is what tenderizes your heart and brings you to a place where he is your number 1 focus and attention. Especially in the times that we are living in now, with disease, sickness, fear, debates, and political frustrations, we must learn how to get away and seek the Lord. If you spend most of your time on social media, conversing with people, watching the news, and filling yourself with the ideology of this world, this will slowly but surely pull you from your first love. It's so challenging for Americans to pray or see breakthrough in their lives because they are filled more with the conversations of the earth rather than the conversation of heaven. You must guard your heart from anything that will pull you from your devotion to God because it is not enough to have a past memory of what God did in your life a long time ago when you first got saved. You must have an everyday walk with the Lord. For many Americans today, this is foreign because they have made Jesus a cherry on top of the ice cream or the icing on the cake, not realizing that Jesus is either all or nothing. You cannot pick and choose how much of the Lord you will have. You must come all the way with him and let him change the core and condition of your heart. When you look at sickness, it affects the body in a way that can do serious harm and even be fatal if not treated, and it all comes from small bacteria that we can't even see. I believe this is exactly how spiritual bacteria gets into our hearts without us knowing it, and before we can catch it, it takes root inside of our hearts, and we begin to go through spiritual sickness that can become fatal to our walk with God. The moment you allow just a little here and there of the world into your heart is like letting sickness into your body that will cause serious symptoms later. You must learn how to run to Doctor Jesus. I'm not saying you have to go away into a bubble and never interact with the world. Obviously, that wouldn't be wise. But what I'm saying is **we must learn how to live in the world without becoming like the world**. You're only healing and protection is in the secret place with the Lord. This is why Psalm 91 says, "Those who dwell in the secret place of the almighty will abide under the shelter of the almighty." Not those who visit the secret place, but those who dwell, meaning this has become a lifestyle for you. You can be going through your day at work, working, joking, having a good time, and immediately the Lord pulls you away to the bathroom to speak to him, and as you get in there and speak to him, everything within you moves and responds to him. Even if this means shutting down your Facebook for some time just to be with the Lord, do what you must do to escape the demonic trap the enemy is placing over believers worldwide. I have seen more believers fighting and arguing through social media than ever before. Everyone has an opinion, idea, or comment to give.

Most of the Christianity that I see on Facebook today does not look like anything I see in the scriptures. We have virtuous, angry, and offended people putting weights on others, arguing every chance they get. Many others are completely addicted and get most of their Christianity from quotes, inspirational posts, and videos rather than a one-on-one relationship with Jesus in a prayer room where no one is looking and where no one can congratulate you or criticize you. I am not saying this to rebuke anyone. I'm just praying and crying out that God's people would return to knowing him in secret. I'm also not against social media because I believe it's an amazing tool for the Lord to share the gospel and his heart with people. I have seen many people healed, delivered, and set free through our social media platform, but the moment it becomes an idol, you must tear it down and get alone with Jesus. Ministry is the same way. The moment you allow doing things for God to replace being with God, you set yourself up for a trap that can even lead you to lawlessness, where you only depend on what you do for the Lord to feel close to him, and that is very dangerous. I believe as you are reading this, God is placing a fire inside of your heart to seek him and be with him. I promise you there is no better place to be in the whole world than to be in the presence of God. The apostle Paul says in Philippians 3:10, "That I might know him and the fellowship of his suffering." This was a man who used to be a top Pharisee before he gave his life to Jesus with much knowledge, experience, and connections. He was making a major impact in many churches and spreading the gospel at a faster rate than others, but he came down to one conclusion that the only thing he truly wanted was to know the Lord and the fellowship of his suffering. The only way you can get to this place is really yielding your heart to the Lord and wanting it more than anything else. You can put two Christians in a room, one who has spent five years of the Christian walk, loving God in secret and doing his will, and another who only knows about God through preaching and church attendance, and then speak to the both of them about how beautiful it is to speak to Jesus alone and spend time with him. One will understand and the other won't because they both have different perspectives of the Christian walk. The word *perspective* means "point of view," meaning it is the way you see a particular thing, place, or person. Perspective is directly connected to your heart and how you see. Ephesians 1:18 speaks about the eyes of our hearts being able to be opened, meaning you have eyes in your heart. Now obviously, he doesn't mean you literally have eyeballs in the organ of your heart, but you have a perspective inside of your soul on how you see everything, and unless that gets renewed, you will always live beneath what God has for you. Whatever your heart is full of is how you see everything. If offense is what fills your heart, then you will always see people through the perspective of what happened to you a long time ago, and you will misunderstand, mislabel, and hurt people who have done nothing wrong. A broken heart can only see brokenness. Therefore, it is of utmost importance to let God replace your heart through intimacy, but not only replace it but also let him fill it. Your perspective of life means everything, because if your perspective of everything is screwed and messed up, you will never truly accomplish the will of the Lord, nor will you be able to see people properly or even the Lord. I have met so many people, even in the church, who see others through their past experiences. These are usually the people who say, "I don't trust anyone." Although there may be a healthy truth in that statement, they are using that as an excuse to remain broken inside. This is why there is a big difference between "instinct" and "Godly discernment."

When you are broken, you will misjudge, mischaracterize, and even hurt other people, sometimes without even knowing it. This is why you have to examine your heart and do a deep inventory of what's in there. You can have things rooted in there from ten years ago, and you didn't even know that they are the reason you've been struggling in some areas. Strongholds start in seed forms and later become giants that you cannot even control anymore. The good news is that God is a giant slayer, and he can and will destroy any and every giant in your life, but you must give them to God wholeheartedly, the same God who split the massive Red Sea for Moses, took down Goliath for David, healed the sick, raised the dead, and opened the blind eyes that live inside of you. Do not let the enemy trick you into believing that you're always going to have strongholds and nothing is going to change. The devil is a liar! Give God your whole heart and watch what he does with it. Many times, we think we can do better with our lives than God. We will never say it from our mouths, but we prove it with our actions. We have zero ability to change what only he can change. You might be able to change your weight, change your diet, change your job, or even change your location, but only Jesus can conquer those demons that have been raging against you. One of the things that I have learned with the Lord is that he does not bargain deals or negotiates terms of peace. He either has everything or nothing at all. Jesus does not want to be your sidepiece or mistress; he must be absolutely your everything. There may be some things that you have been holding on to because you feel like you're not ready to give them up, but I remember the Lord speaking to me awhile back and telling me, "Devon, if you're not ready to lose everything for me, you're not ready to follow me." You need to know that God demands all of your heart, not just some of it. I believe he wants to heal you as you read this and set you free from oppression and strongholds. I pray that God would do it for you right now, in Jesus's mighty name!

* * *

CHAPTER 5

The Time of Your Visitation

Mark 6:6: "He could not do any miracles there, except lay his hands on a few sick people and heal them. He was amazed at their lack of faith. Then Jesus went around teaching from village to village."

When you look at this specific verse, Jesus comes to his hometown (where he grew up) to minister and heal the sick, but the people there do not receive him, so the scripture says, "Because of their lack of faith he could do no miracles there." They had become so familiar with him as a person that they could not see him as who he truly was. They were so blinded by their opinions of him that they couldn't see that their healing and deliverance was right in front of them. Jesus can be in the same room as you, but because of familiarity, you miss him. Becoming too familiar with Jesus can be very dangerous to your walk with him, but most importantly, it can be very dangerous to your visitation with him. Because the people in Nazareth were so used to Jesus, they were unable to get the very things that I'm sure they prayed for, and I believe this is the same with us today. You can pray for revival in your life or revival in your church, and because of familiarity, Jesus can show up, and we completely miss him. This is why holy admiration of Jesus is so important, because God won't bless you beyond your reverence of him. This doesn't mean God doesn't want to bless you. It means that you have to come to a place of honoring him above your knowledge of him. So many Christians have been trapped by what they know of God, and it has robbed them from truly experiencing him. You can spend your whole life reading and studying someone, but until you sit down and speak to them face-to-face, you will never truly know them. Knowledge and experience are two completely different things. God wants to change your heart's direction. Many times our heart is directed toward the things of God rather than God himself, and this can become dangerous. There have been many times in my life where I began to depend on what I knew of God rather than coming to a place of dependency. There are many Christians who live in a place of independence, and I believe God wants to completely crush that. Independence tells God that you have everything under control and you have him all figured out. The moment you allow the mindset of independence to come in, you close every avenue for the Holy Spirit to work in your life. You cannot merely depend on what you have or what you had; you must be desperate and dependent on him every day for something new. Those who are dependent on him are those who will always live a life of experience. To be dependent means to completely rely or be determined by "another." You must come to a place of completely yielding to the Holy Spirit that you rely on Jesus for everything. In this place, and only in this place, can you truly experience him when he shows up.

Jesus tells the disciples in Acts 1:4 not to leave Jerusalem but wait for the promised Holy Spirit, but I wonder what would have happened if they did not wait for the Holy Spirit and they missed their time of visitation from God and depended on what they had in the past with Jesus. I believe you can fall into the trap of operating your Christianity off residue. You might be wondering what I mean by that. Well, let's look at what the word means. The word *residue* means "a small amount of something that remains after the main part has gone or been taken away or used." You can operate out of the leftover of what you once received in truth and dependency and begin to make for yourself a Christianity of independence. God wants us to constantly live in a life of flow, and this is how you can sense him moving in your life and know when he is close. You are left with the idea of Christ and not the revelation of Christ, merely holding on to what to know rather than a fresh encounter.

Independent Christianity can get you a lot of knowledge, but knowledge and revelation are two completely different words. Knowledge is what you learn on your own or what someone teaches you. Revelation is what is revealed to you by the Father. Therefore, the book of Revelation is not called the book of knowledge because it was by revelation from the spirit of God that showed John everything he had seen and heard. Unless the Father reveals Jesus to us, we will continue looking at him as a Sunday service, Bible study, or historical figure, but he is so much more than all of that. You cannot put the creator of the universe in a box. There is no mindset or idea that can hold all that God is. Many times in our churches, in our lives, and even in what we do for the Lord, we attempt to put God in a box and lock it with justifications such as "God doesn't do it like that anymore,'" "It doesn't take all of that," or "That's not protocol." We have to be careful without religiosity because it was that same religiosity that called the Pharisees to miss God when he was walking among them and speaking to them face-to-face. They missed what God was doing in the earth because they depended on religiosity locked in a box. God cannot be contained, nor can you control what he does or what he wants to do. The Bible says God chose the foolish things of the world to shame the wise; God chose the weak things of the world to shame the strong. God will raise the very person we disregard and overlook and will show up in a way that is below what we expected. Jesus came and took the lowly position of a servant, and this is why they missed their visitation with him because he came in the form of something they disregarded and thought nothing of. Think of what happens when familiarity happens. Let us say you buy a brand-new couch and get rid of your old one. Immediately, you become satisfied and excited about it and treat it with respect and care. Now let's say seven years goes by. After a while, you will eventually become familiar with that couch and won't have the same respect and satisfaction you had when you first got it. Why? Because you became too familiar with it. Don't become so familiar that you stop giving God the honor and respect that he deserves.

Every time you encounter God, you encounter what you are here for. When you see Jesus, you see the purpose for why you're alive all at the same time. Jesus embodies your salvation, redemption, healing, and purpose. This is why every time Jesus showed up in a town, the people of that town would flock around him, and there was always a remnant of those people who were willing to go to any measure to get to him, even if it cost them popularity or reputation, because they understood that their window of opportunity to experience him was opened and they had to take it. There were many who missed their opportunity because of ignorance, misunderstanding, and lack of faith, but there was also a group of people who were willing to risk their very own lives just to get to him. Most of them had never seen him a day in their life, but something inside of them yearned for him; something inside of them felt undone and incomplete without him. Some of them had no verses or scriptures to tell them who he was or a preacher to break it down to them; they just had an unquenchable desire to meet him, fueled with conviction and zeal.

I can just imagine someone telling the woman with the issue of blood in Luke 8:43 that Jesus was in town and her freezing in place, thinking, "This may be my only chance to see the one who embodies why I'm alive, the one who can fix what has been broken. I must go to him, or I will live the rest of my life with the burden of guilt, regret, and shame. I must go see him!" In that time, when Jesus would show up, many people would crowd around him, sometimes by the hundreds or even thousands. It was very difficult to get to Jesus when he was in town. Everyone was interested to hear him speak or even just to be around him. The religious came to test him, the sick came to be healed, the oppressed came to be set free, and the poor came to hear him speak. I can just imagine this woman who had this condition in her body for twelve years hearing that Jesus was nearby and seeing how many people crowded him and she still decided to go after him no matter the hindrance that was in front of her. She was desperate to seize her window of opportunity. The Bible says that she touched the hem of his garment, which was the lowest part of his robe, meaning she had to be on her hands and knees. This indicates that there were so many people around Jesus that she could not stand and touch him. She had to crawl underneath everyone just to get to him. This not only reveals how much faith she had to be healed but also shows her level of dedication and passion for the Lord. It is believed that she had never met Jesus in her life based on the conversation they had and the moral of the story, so this is what makes this story so much more powerful and transformational when you really think about it. All she had were the stories of Jesus and the notification that he was in town, and that was enough for her to lay down her entire life and go after him. We must be willing to lay down our very own lives to take advantage of the window of opportunity open to us to follow the Lord and his purpose for our lives. Many times God will come to you through a dream, a vision, or a person to lay out the will for your life, but you have to be hungry enough to grab hold of it when he shows you. There are so many people whom God has revealed himself to or revealed his will for their lives, but they continue to live for themselves and run from the Lord's will. Sometimes it becomes so comfortable to live like everyone else and make Jesus just an add-on. But God is calling us to be desperate for him and his purpose for our lives that we are even willing to be uncomfortable and endure hardship. This is why Jesus says you must count the cost of what it is to be a disciple because there is a cost to pay to truly walk for God. It's not always going to be sunshine and flowers. You're going to go through situations when you finally come to the place of following the Lord and going after his purpose for your life. The enemy will throw every and any type of trial your way to stop you or slow you down, but you have to be willing to break through the crowd like the woman with the issue of blood and reach out for Jesus in the midst of your trials. The door of opportunity that God has given you to follow him must be used. Even as you are reading this book, I believe God is visiting you through the very words that are written, and you have to make a decision in your heart to truly follow the Lord and do what he is telling you to do. I guarantee right now I have people reading this book who are called to be ministers, missionaries, pastors, prophets, evangelists, book writers, dancers, and more, but because of comfortability and familiarity, you have walked right past the door that was open for you, and you continue to live in a place of comfort. You have to understand that when God calls you, he does not call you to be comfortable. He will disrupt your whole life just to get your attention and put you on a narrow path that many times looks like a rock and a hard place. He does not promise that everything will be easy, but he promises that he will never leave us or forsake us. He has given us the greatest promise of all that his presence will go with us through hardship. Don't ever let a bad day determine your future with God. You must only hear the voice of the Father calling you to greater heights. The devil's job is to steal kill and destroy. The more you hear his voice, he will steal every ounce of passion you have to go after God. He tends to come as the loudest voice in your life, trying to overpower the voice of the Father. God always comes as a still small voice, but the moment you hear a scream or yelling, that is the enemy trying to lead you away from where God is calling you. The moment you distinguish the difference between the Lord and the enemy, you will be able to proper resist the devil. This is why James 4 says, "Submit to God. Resist the devil and he will flee from you," because the power to resist the devil comes from your submission to God. If you are not willing to submit to God when he calls, you have no power to resist the enemy that is trying to steal, kill, and destroy you. Hebrews 3:15 says, "If you hear his voice, do not harden your hearts as you did in the rebellion." The moment you hear his calling in your heart, be it through a dream, a book, a preaching, or a conversation, you must immediately submit yourself to God. As you give God your full and undivided devotion, he comes to support you and will deliver you from the oppressor.

In Luke 19:44, Jesus begins to weep over Jerusalem and makes a prophecy that disaster would come upon the city and the people. He tells them that if only they knew that this was their time of peace, they would have been able to walk in it, but they denied Jesus, not knowing who he was. He then later says, "All these things will happen to you because you did not know the time of your visitation." The most important call we will ever receive is the call of the Lord, and we must all respond to it. However, many do not believe and have become so comfortable with their lives. There are even Christians who have prayed the prayer and go to church every day but still have not answered the call of God over their lives. They begin to see Jesus as just another part of their lives, and he becomes something they do on Sunday or during Bible study, and they live the rest of their lives never answering that call. When it's your time, it's your time, and you have to be willing to go after it with all of your heart like that woman with the issue of blood. She did not care who would come against her or how she would look. She only wanted to touch the one who could truly restore her. The Bible says that she had previously seen many doctors but none of them could help her. When Jesus comes into your life, he often comes at a time when you have tried every other option and nothing has worked, so you must be willing to deny yourself and follow him. If I would have missed the call of God ten years ago, I don't know where I would be or who I would be. All I know is that I would be a complete mess. Even if I had accomplished a lot financially, none of it would matter if I did not follow the will of the Lord. You can live your whole life reaching the greatest achievements and winning the approval of everyone, but if you do not follow the will of God for your life, on the day of judgment, all of your accomplishments will be burned in the fire, and the only thing left will be you and him face-to-face. On that day, none of us will have an excuse for the decisions we made, but we all have a chance right now to lay our lives down and answer the call.

I love this story of Zacchaeus. He truly models for us how far one is willing to go, even in being in a place where he knows the Jews do not respect him. I'm sure that in his heart, he probably felt bad about all that he had done before he climbed that tree. But he was willing to do everything and anything he could do to seize his moment of visitation. There are many times when Jesus will show up in your life like how he showed up in Zacchaeus's life. But because Zac had the tenacity and the drive to go to any extent just to see him, Jesus walked by and invited himself in Zacchaeus's home. The question is, what are you willing to risk? Or what measure are you willing to go to seize your moment with Jesus? I believe we have free access to Jesus every single day because of his shed blood on the cross, but there are divine moments in your life when God begins to move sovereignty in your life and you have to jump on board and not miss that moment. There have been times when I felt strongly that God wanted me to do something and I waited and then went to do it and nothing happened, but there also have been moments when I felt strongly to do something and I did it and saw the glory and power of God in amazing ways. Partial obedience is still disobedience. You must follow his lead the first time. He loves you and will always give you a second chance, but you must learn how to move when he moves. There is so much power in following God the first time and not making your life more difficult because of disobedience. I don't believe that Zacchaeus climbing that tree was his own doing. I believe he was obeying the voice of the Lord in his heart that told him to climb the tree. Have you ever had moments in your life when you heard a "still small" voice tell you to go there, do this, or speak to that person? Many times God comes like a still small voice during all the commotion of life. In the book of Kings, Elijah, the prophet, was found running from an evil woman by the name of Jezebel (the wife of King Ahab). After Elijah had confronted the false prophets of Baal, he prayed to God, and the Lord sent fire down to consume them. Jezebel was filled with anger because she supported these false prophets, so she threatened the life of Elijah. This sent Elijah running to the wilderness. All Elijah did was the will of the Lord, and this caused him to be threatened and chased by the enemy. Many times your obedience to God will make you a target for the enemy. Your attendance in church does not threaten the devil, nor does your profession of Jesus. It is your obedience to God that scares him. Therefore, Peter writes to the church, "Dear friends, do not be surprised at the fiery ordeal that has come on you to test you, as though something strange were happening to you." He tells them to not even be surprised when things come against us because this is an announcement that you belong to Christ. Even Christ suffered for obedience. If nothing is coming against you, I question if you are truly obeying the Lord, because when you truly do what God wants you to do, all of hell will rise against you, but I thank God that we serve a faithful God who sees all things and has his hand on our lives!

1 Kings 19:11–12

The LORD said, "Go out and stand on the mountain in the presence of the LORD, for the LORD is about to pass by." Then a great and powerful wind tore the mountains apart and shattered the rocks before the LORD, but the LORD was not in the wind. After the wind there was an earthquake, but the LORD was not in the earthquake. After the earthquake came a fire, but the LORD was not in the fire. And after the fire came a gentle whisper.

Elijah saw fire go before him, but God was not in the first. He said wind, and God was not in the wind. He saw an earthquake, but God was not in the earthquake. But then a still small voice came, and Elijah knew it was the Lord and wrapped his cloak around himself. God does not always come in the way you want him to come. Therefore, you have to be careful with becoming familiar with how he moved in the past. This is why Jesus says unless you become like a little child, you will, by no means, see the kingdom of God because the kingdom of God does not always look how you want it to look. You must have faith like a child that is willing to believe anything and accept whatever form it comes in. So Elijah recognized his time of visitation, and he responded to the Lord. After he heard that still small voice, God spoke to him and told him where he needed to go and what he needed to do. Don't miss your instructions because you're so busy running from demons and caught up in everyday life. Elijah could have used Jezebel as an excuse to be distracted, but he instead obeyed the voice of the Lord and waited for God's voice and responded by going where he wanted him to go and doing what he wanted him to do. You cannot expect God's blessing to shower down on you while you stand in a place of disobedience. You must hear his voice and respond immediately. There are so many doctors who are called to the mission field but have denied the call. There are so many pastors who are called to be traveling prophets but refuse to follow the instruction of God over their lives. You would be freer if you would just follow his instructions for your life. I believe we all have a book in heaven not only with our deeds but also with the instructions of our life written before we were even born. We must seek the Lord to find out why we are here and what we are called to do. Jesus said in the gospels, "I seek not my own will, but the will of the Father." Even Jesus had to get alone in prayer and seek God's will for his life. But we have so many people who would rather do what they want to do or what seems acceptable. You can do what pleases people, or you can do what pleases God. It's your choice.

Trust me, I get it. There are going to be attacks in your life that try to stray you from where God has you, but even Elijah had that problem and knew he had to get back on track. Elijah was following God's will for his life when he was prophesying to kings and battling the false prophets of Baal, but when Jezebel showed up, she completely took Elijah off track and had him hiding in caves when he should have been ministering to kings. There are places in your life where the enemy has you hiding in caves instead of doing what you were called and created to do. Don't allow the cares of life and the distractions of the day to mislead you. The enemy is very subtle and sneaky, and he will do everything and anything he can to bring you to a place of despair and hopelessness. Jesus says the devil is a liar, and when he speaks, he speaks his native language which is a lie. He doesn't know what else to do but lie. It's who he is, and he will use his crafty gift of lying to mislead you away from your visitation with the Lord and where you are headed. You must choose to lay aside every distraction and grab hold of Jesus and his purpose for your life no matter what it costs you.

CHAPTER 6

Relationship with the Holy Spirit

This chapter was written by my wife, Franceska Maddox.

"If you **love** me, keep my commands. And I will ask the Father, and he will give you another advocate to help you and be with you **forever** the Spirit of truth. The world cannot accept him, because it neither sees him nor knows him. But you know him, for he lives with you and will be in you. I will not leave you as orphans; I will come to you. Before long, the world will not see me anymore, but you will see me. Because I live, you also will live. On that day you will realize that I am in my Father, and you are in me, and I am in you. Whoever has my commands and keeps them is the one who loves me. The one who loves me will be loved by my Father, and I too will love them and show myself to them." —John 14:15–21

A relationship with the Holy Spirit is vital. He is important. He is everything. Without him, we are nothing. The Holy Spirit is so precious and so wonderful. He is our comforter, our strength, our teacher, and so much more. We must acknowledge his presence and KNOW that he is truly with us. We all know that a relationship takes time. You have to connect with the Holy Spirit DAILY. Get to know him. Enjoy fellowship with him. He has feelings. It is important to

---

hear from the Holy Spirit so he can guide you throughout your day. God has a task for all of us to accomplish every day, so it is important to take that time and allow the Holy Spirit to talk to you. I like to wake up in the morning and say, "Good morning, Holy Spirit. How are you today?" Then I like to thank him for waking me up in the morning and ask him for strength to get through the day. I know that life can get pretty busy. I just want to sit down with the Father all day if I can, but I am also a busy mother and wife, so it can get a little challenging to sit down how I would really like to. But the good news is that Holy Spirit lives in you. Now you do need to take some time to soak in the Spirit and be in the secret place with God. But it doesn't mean that when we have to do life, we put Jesus in a closet and go about our day. He is with us always. Isaiah 41:10 says, **"So do not fear, for I am with you; do not be dismayed, for I am your God. I will strengthen you and help you; I will uphold you with my righteous right hand."** So while you are doing the dishes, cleaning, cooking, or taking care of your children, he is also there, which is so amazing. When you set your sights on him while you are doing life, everything changes. You can still spend time with the Lord throughout your busy daily schedule. We have literally connected the Holy Spirit to a room or a church, but he is with us all the time. I like to go throughout my day KNOWING that the Holy Spirit is with me. He is our father and friend.

The Holy Spirit wants your attention. He loves you. He wants to spend time with you, and he wants you to spend time with him throughout your day. He longs for you. If you think about a relationship with someone you love, whether it is your spouse or your children, how would you feel if this individual never spoke to you or only spoke to you when they wanted something from you? Or what if they only spoke to you once a week? Can you go a day without hearing your loved one say "I love you"? The same goes for the Holy Spirit. He loves when we converse with him. Communication is key in any relationship. How much more if it is communication with the Holy Spirit, our Father, the one who created us in his image?

Do Not Grieve the Holy Spirit

And do not grieve the Holy Spirit of God, by whom
you were **sealed** for the day of redemption.

—Ephesians 4:30

**We grieve the Holy Spirit by walking in the flesh, holding on to
bitterness, rage, anger, gossip, and any form of malice. We need
to protect our ear gates and eye gates. The enemy can come in by
what you hear and by what you watch. We must be careful what we
allow into our heart and soul. Those things can go deep into our
soul and create roots that don't belong.**

Do not allow anything or anyone get in the way of your relationship.
There are so many things that the enemy will try to present and
throw your way to try to come in between your relationship with
God. We live in a world full of distractions. Why did Adam and Eve
fall? They allowed distraction to get in the way. That distraction
caused them to disobey the will of God. The Lord walked into the
garden and asked, "Where are you?" When he asked that question,
I believe he asked, "What did you allow to get in between our
relationship?" I want us to take a moment and think about what
things have we allowed to get in the way. Please pray with me.
**"Heavenly Father, I ask that you forgive me for anything that I
have allowed to get in the way of our relationship. I pray that you
forgive me and that you restore our relationship and help me get
closer to you in Jesus's name. Amen."**

The Holy Spirit desires intimacy with us. We need to have that
intimate relationship with the Holy Spirit and not grieve him by
ignoring him when he is trying to spend time with us. The Holy
Spirit is so precious. He longs for our conversation. He longs for
us to talk to him and worship him. We need to be aware of his
presence. Do not ignore him when he tries to spend time with

you. He loves you. You are his precious child. Intimacy with the Lord is such a beautiful thing. In those moments, you experience Jesus for who he truly is, and in it, there is transformation through his love.

Obedience

God gives the Holy Spirit to those who obey him. —Acts 5:32

The Lord wants your obedience. (Obedience is
better than sacrifices.) —1 Samuel 15:2

When you love Jesus and you have a revelation of his love for you, your desires change. You just want to obey and do the will of God for your life. Being a follower of Christ is based on obedience, laying down your life for the one who laid his down for you. Laying down your life is giving your all to Jesus, denying yourself, picking up your cross, and following him. We are now his children (Romans 8:14). We received the spirit of adoption. If you are a parent, you would want your children to obey you. It is a sign of respect, honor, and love. When disobedience comes in, we discipline our kids for making the wrong decisions. We still love them, but there are consequences for the bad decisions that they made. The same goes for us. As God's children, we must obey the Holy Spirit when he leads us. We must also walk this walk faithfully and commit to our Heavenly Father because there are consequences for our disobedience. God chastises those he loves (Hebrews 12:6). We must walk in obedience. We don't walk as orphans anymore. We walk as children, knowing that the Holy Spirit is with us and sees and hears everything. When the Lord says GO, you must go. If the Lord says no, don't do this, or yes, do that, we need to follow his lead. We must live our daily lives knowing that the eyes of his spirit are on us. When we walk in the spirit, we will not have the desire to walk in the things of the flesh. When you are led by the spirit, you discover who you truly are in

Christ, and we must know who we are in Christ. This is extremely vital. If we walk around not knowing who we are, we give room for lies and deception to creep in. We must know our identity in him. We must know that he loves us and is for us. We must know that we can do all things through Christ who strengthens us.

The Holy Spirit is the most important gift for a Christian believer after their salvation. Many people connect the Holy Spirit to power, which, in many cases, is true. Without the direct empowerment of the Holy Spirit, no miracle can be done. But the Holy Spirit is much more than power. When Jesus was on earth, the disciples had built an everlasting covenant and relationship with him that I can imagine was very close. They faithfully walked with Jesus for three years, traveling from region to region, holding conversations that we don't talk about today because they were never recorded. Intimate and emotional conversations that one can only imagine. We get a glimpse of their relationship by the questions they asked Jesus and the response they had to his statements. A lot of the questions and statements they made to Jesus would be considered "comfortable" questions and statements, meaning they would be comfortable enough with Jesus to speak to him the way they did, and this can only come about through an intimate relationship with him where you know him and he knows you. The Holy Spirit does not only come to give you empowerment. He comes to be a helper, comforter, advocate, intercessor-counselor, strengthener, and standby, according to John 14:26. In your time of weakness, the Holy Spirit is there to strengthen you, but many believers ignore this important part of the God head. The Holy Spirit wants to intimately speak with you and reveal the nature of Jesus to you. Communion with the Holy Spirit is what will mark you and separate you from others who only have the name "Christian" without the life. The purpose of the Lord over your life is to mark you and make you different from everyone else. This is why Moses said, "Lord, unless you go with us, we will not go. How will they know we are different?" The only thing that makes you different is the presence of God over your life. The Holy Spirit in you and on you is what distinguishes you from everyone else. The Holy Spirit marks you, and this mark reveals that you belong to Him. The word *mark* means to be "evident" or "clearly seen." This is an evident sign that God is with you, that you are marked by the Holy Spirit. This is what changes your life inside and out, and without the mark of the Holy Spirit on your life, you merely only have a claim without the evidence.

This is why Paul says in 1 Corinthians 2:4, "My message and my preaching were not with wise and persuasive words, but with a demonstration of the Spirit's power." The demonstration of the Holy Spirit's power is a part of God's mark on your life, and this will show the world that you belong to him. My prayer is that God would raise a generation of people who have an intimate relationship with the Holy Spirit and are eternally marked by him. Many people are speaking of being marked by the beast. My only concern is are we marked by the Holy Spirit. The devil is a cheap imitator of God, and he tries to copy everything that God is. So if the devil has a mark, you better believe God has a mark for his children, and I believe it's the Holy Spirit resting on your life.

As a wife, I'm a cleaner. I love to clean. When I clean, I take everything that is hiding, any clutter, anything that I might not need anymore, out first. Then from there, I toss out, donate, or organize what I have to. But in the process, the house will look completely destroyed because of everything that I took out. I like to dig deep and clean thoroughly. I look at my husband and tell him that it looks messy now but wait until I'm finished; it will be super clean and organized. I tell him that this is how I clean and to not panic when he sees the mess. He looks at me and smiles. When I'm done, everything is nice, clean, and organized. One day, as I was cleaning, doing what I do, I felt the Holy Spirit say, "This is what I do with you. I dig deep. I take out all the things that don't belong. I organize you, and I clean you from the inside out. It might not feel or look the way you might want it at first. It will feel uncomfortable. It will look messy. But when I am done with you, you will be able to see the whole picture. You will be able to see what I have done with you. You will be clean not just from the outside, but from the inside out!" This revelation hit me hard, and I thanked the Holy Spirit so much for doing what he has been doing with me. My prayer now is "Lord, remove the things that are in me that don't belong. You see all things, even things that are hidden that I might not know about. Lord, remove these things because you know my house (my temple). You created me in your image. You made me, and you know what should be in there and what should not. I love you, Lord." He is my father. He is Abba. He loves us so much that he wants to not only have us look clean on the outside. He wants to get deep within us and clean us from the inside so we can shine on the outside!

To All Women

For moms who feel like they don't have the time to spend with the Lord or do anything for him, yes, we can. While we cook, while we clean, while we handle our children, we can talk to the Holy Spirit and spend time with him. Did you know that our first ministry is our homes? Our children, our husbands, even our house. While we do what we do as mothers, as wives, we are doing it as we are doing it unto the Lord.

> "Work willingly at whatever you do, as though you were working for the Lord rather than for people." —Colossians 3:23

I encourage you to wake up early in the morning before anyone at home wakes up to give the Lord the first fruits of your day. Spend time with the Lord, and everything else through the day will fall into place.

Even busy mothers who work and come home to be a mom and a wife or even single moms, you still can spend time with the Lord at work. Speak to him in your mind take him to work with you every day. Take time on your break or bathroom break to say, "I love u, Jesus." While you are working, ask the Holy Spirit, "Is there anyone you want me to talk to today at work?" Say, "Lord, I am listening," and he will lead you and guide you on what he wants you to do. Stay in tune with the Holy Spirit at all times. Don't leave the Holy Spirit at home while you go to work. Take him everywhere you go. Acknowledge that he is in you and he is with you.

> "I am with you always, *even* unto the end of
> the world. Amen." —Matthew 28:20

CHAPTER 7

Eternity and Judgment Day

Hebrews 9:27

"And just as it is appointed for man to die
once, and after that comes judgment."

Many times I wonder if we have forgotten the humbling truth of judgment day, the day where every knee will bow (Romans 14:11), where every motive and hidden thought will be laid bare (1 Corinthians 4:5 and Romans 2:16). Paul says in 2 Corinthians 5:10, "For we must all appear before the judgment seat of Christ, so that each one may receive what is due for what he has done in the body, whether good or evil."

As far as the eye can see and beyond that, you will see billions upon billions like the ocean spreading across the earth of people standing to be judged from all walks of life and all generations who have ever lived. You will see people of all ages, races, cultures, religions, and economic status. Presidents, kings, pharaohs, government officials, CEOs, nurses, doctors, and so many more looking to the one whose face shines like the sun, whose eyes blazes like fire, and whose his head is crowned with many crowns, symbolizing that he is the king

---

of kings and the lord of lords, according to Revelation 19:12. There will be no sounds of people arguing, debating, or trying to find out what is happening because everyone will see him and know that this is the time of judgment. In that moment, no one will be able to argue simply because everything will be laid bare. You won't have the ability to argue your point or defend your life while looking in the eyes of the one who knows it all. On earth, you could hide, lie, and debate, but on that day, there is no room for that, nor would you even want to attempt it. Everyone's life will flash before their eyes one by one as they approach the judgment seat of Christ, according to 2 Corinthians 5:10. This will be a day of great gain and great loss, according to 1 Corinthians 3:15, a day of victory and a day of defeat. It all depends on which side of the line you are standing on. One of the most important things to understand on this day is that everyone had a chance to do all that God created them to do and no one will have an excuse. Romans 1:18 says,

"For what can be known about God is plain to them because God has shown it to them. For his invisible attributes, namely, his eternal power and divine nature, have been clearly perceived, ever since the creation of the world, in the things that have been made. So, they are without excuse. For although they knew God, they did not honor him as God or give thanks to him, but they became futile in their thinking, and their foolish hearts were darkened."

No one on that day can say they did not believe in God or that they did not know because the Lord has revealed himself to everyone, even through creation. On this final day of judgment, everything will be revealed pertaining to the life that we lived, the decisions we made, the secrets we kept, the lies we told, the truth we told, the good deeds and bad deeds we did. Everything will be laid out in the open. The only dominance and forgiveness will come through the blood of Jesus, and if you did not accept God's free gift, there will be no forgiveness on that day. On that day, you will not be able to get a lawyer or representative of the court to help uphold your case or get you a lower sentence. Every person will stand for one final judgment, but those who had accepted the free gift of Jesus Christ will, in other words, have Jesus as their lawyer. He is the only way, the only truth, and the only life, and on that day, his full nature and character will also be revealed to all, and everyone will know that he is that he is. Right now, we have false teachers saying that there are many ways, but on that day, you will see that Jesus was and will always be the only way, the only truth, and the only life.

Another key point to understand is that even believers will come to be judged according to their works. Some will have great loss and others great gain.

1 Corinthians 3:13

"Their work will be shown for what it is because the Day will bring it to light. It will be revealed with fire, and the fire will test the quality of each person's work. If what has been built survives, the builder will receive a reward. If it is burned up, the builder will suffer loss but will be saved— even though only as one escaping through the flames."

Everything that you built in life that was not directly inspired by the Lord will be burned. This means everything that was done, from the city you lived in to the job you worked, to the ministry you did and every work of your hands, if you were not directly led by the Lord to do it, on that day, you will suffer loss because all of it will be burned, and the only thing that will survive is everything that was inspired by the Lord. This verse gives clarity that many will suffer great loss but also make it to heaven literally by the skin of their teeth. Just because you suffer great loss does not mean you are counted among those who are cast out. It says "as one escaping through the flames," meaning you just made it by the end of your life. So your only reward would be heaven, but there are those who accomplished a lot for the Lord who will be greatly rewarded, from preaching the gospel, winning souls for Jesus, and feeding the poor to building organizations and ministries that help minister the word and help others. Every selfless act that you did to help grow the kingdom of God, from worship songs to books you wrote, will be rewarded. There will be great rewards. James 1:12 says, "For those who have suffered much will receive the crown of life." This implies that there will be gifts given to those who obeyed the Lord and were faithful to the very end. In Luke 12, Jesus says, "Store up treasures in heaven." This implies that you have the ability through obedience to God and serving others to store up for yourself treasures in heaven that will be given to you on that day. In 2 Timothy 4:8, it says,

"Henceforth there is laid up for me the crown of righteousness, which the Lord, the righteous judge, will award to me on that Day, and not only to me but also to all who have loved his appearing."

This specific crown is for those who lived righteously because they longed for his coming. He will crown them with the crown of righteousness. It is amazing to think of the great blessings that await us when this life is over and how beautiful it will be when the Lord looks at you with satisfaction and joy, knowing that you endured to the very end. Although we will be blessed with the treasures of heaven, the greatest gift will be to look in the eyes of Jesus and know that on that day, he is pleased with you. I promise you on that day there will be nothing greater than to know you are right with God. There are only two statements that we will hear on that day, and they are "Well done, good and faithful servant!" or "Depart from me I never knew you."

It is so important to do what God called you to do no matter what it costs you, because when you stand before the Lord, the only things that will matter will pertain to what he called you to do and if you had a relationship with him. These are two major factors on the day of judgment. Although there will be rewards for those who did the will of the father, there will be great loss and even terrifying separation for all who disobeyed the Lord and lived a lifestyle of sin. We are saved by grace and not by works, but salvation looks like a transformed life through repentance. Having received the free gift of Jesus Christ will be of most importance on that day, FOLLOWED BY a life of repentance through a relationship with Jesus.

It cannot merely be what you did for him. It must be that you truly had an authentic relationship with him. Jesus says in Matthew 7:21–23,

> "On that day many will say to me, 'Lord, Lord, did
> we not prophesy in your name, and cast out demons in
> your name, and do many mighty works in your name?'
> And then will I declare to them, 'I never knew you;
> depart from me, you workers of lawlessness.'"

What Jesus is saying is that many will come to him on that day, trying to brag about what they did for him, but the books of their life will reveal that they did not have a relationship with him, and he uses the word *lawlessness*, implying that these individuals did a lot for God but lived a life of sin and darkness and they thought that their great works would save them. But your works will not save you. It is only through faith in Christ, followed by a life of repentance. When you truly love Jesus and have a relationship with him, you won't ever want to violate that covenant relationship. This does not mean he expects you to be perfect because we all fall short of the glory of God, but you must have a relationship with him that is real. You should really love him. Even when you fell into sin, you got right back up and kept following him. But those who lived in sin with no conviction will have to answer for those deeds on the day of judgment. There are many in the church today who believe with all of their heart that they are saved, but according to Matthew 7:21, many of these people will be eternally cast out of the presence of God. Jesus said, "Not everyone who says to me, 'Lord, Lord,' will enter the kingdom of God, but only those who do the will of the Father." Many people are outside of the will of God but believe they are right with God, and this is a strong deception that is falling on the church today. You cannot live a lifestyle of sin and immorality and still expect to make it to heaven. In 1 Corinthians 6:9, it says, "Or do you not know that wrongdoers will not inherit the kingdom of God? Do not be deceived: Neither the sexually immoral nor idolaters nor adulterers nor men who have sex with men nor thieves nor the greedy nor drunkards nor slanderers nor swindlers will inherit the kingdom of God." This is why judgment day is considered the great and terrible day of the Lord, according to Joel 2:31 and Acts 2:20, because on that day, it will be great for

Salvation is given only through faith in Christ, and when you come to that place of putting your faith in him, he gives you instructions for what to do on earth. There are many Christians who are promised heaven, but a lot of their work on earth that was not done in his name will be burned up, and they will inherit heaven but suffer loss. Imagine making it to the gate of heaven and the Lord looking at you and saying, "Come in, but just before I let you in, let me show you all the things you could have done in my name if you would have just trusted me and followed my lead." Heaven cannot be the only goal for Christians. It must also be to complete the work in which he has put us on earth.

Acts 20:24

"However, I consider my life worth nothing to me; my only aim is to finish the race and complete the task the Lord Jesus has given me—the task of testifying to the good news of God's grace."

Now in this verse, Paul is speaking to the elders of the church who were convincing him not to go to Jerusalem, because if he went, they were going to arrest him and possibly have him killed for spreading the gospel. The apostle Paul was a huge threat to the religious system at that time, and it was very dangerous for him to travel to Jerusalem. A lot of the people of God did all they could to convince

Paul not to go, even though God had told him to go. There was even a prophet who came and prophesied everything that was going to happen to him when he got there, concerning him being arrested and taken prisoner, but Paul still said, "I have to go. I consider my life worth nothing to me only to finish my race and do the work of the Lord." Because of Paul, the gospel was able to spread in areas that the church was afraid to travel to, causing the name of Jesus to be brought to all people throughout generations after he died. Because of Paul's obedience, we have the New Testament. He was responsible for writing most of it. Paul's life is an amazing picture and outline for obeying the Lord and completing the work given to you to do. If there was anyone in the Bible who suffered for doing good, it was Paul, yet he continued to do what God called him to do. I can only imagine the eternal reward given to the apostle Paul when he stood before Jesus. There will be times in your walk with God that the Lord is going to tell you to do things that are not popular or well supported by the people around you. You have to be willing to follow God before you ever follow man. Your obedience must be to the Lord first!

It kind of scares me to see a generation rising that does not know what it truly means to lay their lives down for Jesus through obedience. Jesus says, "Anyone who wants to follow me must first deny themselves, pick up their cross, and follow me." This is not just a cute Christian message on Sunday. This is the call of God for every single person who wants to walk this walk to completely deny themselves and follow the Lord even if it costs them popularity, promotion, or even their lives. Paul knew that many would come against him in the church for the decision he was going to make. But not only that, he also knew that he was going to be persecuted and harmed by the people he was going to in Jerusalem. He was receiving attacks from both sides of the spectrum, and I can imagine how much he needed to depend on the Lord for strength and guidance. He concluded that his life laid down for Jesus was more important than anything else this world could give. He did not live for temporary pleasures of acceptance or pleasure. He lived to do the will of the Lord!

I believe we are living in the last days, and with everything that is happening in the world, God is raising an end-time remnant of believers who will go to any extent to accomplish the will of the Lord for their lives. In the beginning of 2020, we had a cluster of major events taking place all at once, from the rumors of war to the fires in Australia, to the massive earthquakes all around the world, to the COVID-19 effecting every country. This is a sign from heaven that we are approaching the day of the Lord a lot sooner than we think. We have always had events similar to these ones in history, but the only difference now is that all these events are happening at once. Deception of doctrines, increase of knowledge and technology, rumors of war, tension between nation, offence arising like never before through social media and within the church, earthquakes, pestilences and disease, increase of prophetic dreams, children prophesying, I can go on and on, but all of these are happening at once throughout the world. The earth is groaning and moaning, waiting for the sons and daughters of God to be made manifest. Prophecies are being fulfilled from the Middle East and throughout the earth, and we must catch the signals from heaven to rise and do all that God has called us to do. If there is a vision in your heart, you must obey the Lord and finish the work of the Lord. There will be many other signs to come and other worldwide events, but we cannot prolong and procrastinate any longer. No matter where you have been, where you grew up, your cultural background, your mistakes, your economic status, you must do the will of the Lord for your life. Jesus is our savior, and his love is bigger than your mistakes and background. He wants to not only change your life but also send you out to do his will. There are people in the world who are waiting for you to rise and do what you were called to do, and unless you do it, they will remain in darkness. I believe the person reading this right now has a major call over their life, and after reading this book, your heart is longing for more of God. Now is the time for you to live wholeheartedly for God with no compromise. If there was ever a time to come to Jesus, now is that time. Never forget that Jesus loves you and he will always be with you.

NOW IS THE TIME.

* * *